P9-CEU-695

OLD BOSTON POST RD.
OLD SAYBROOK
CT 06475
860/395-3184

DATE DUE

JUL 23 2013	
SEP 03 2013	
JUL 24 2014	

BRODART, CO.   Cat. No. 23-221

How Do You Know It's Summer?

Signs of the Seasons

by
Ruth Owen

Consultants:

Suzy Gazlay, MA
Recipient, Presidential Award for Excellence in Science Teaching

Kimberly Brenneman, PhD
National Institute for Early Education Research,
Rutgers University, New Brunswick, New Jersey

BEARPORT
PUBLISHING

New York, New York

Credits

Cover, © MarkMirror/Shutterstock, Alex Smith/Shutterstock, Rolf Nussbaumer/FLPA, Timmary/Shutterstock, Catcher of Light, Inc./Shutterstock; 4, © Vilor/Shutterstock; 5, © MaszaS/Shutterstock; 6L, © Anatoily Samara/Shutterstock; 6, © Lakov Kalinin/Shutterstock; 7, © Corbis/Superstock; 8, © Yellowj/Shutterstock; 8L, © Nordic Photos/Superstock; 9, © Fesus Robert/Shutterstock; 10, © Shutterstock; 11, © Peter Hansen/Shutterstock; 12TL, © Dani Vincek/Shutterstock; 12BL, © Ulrich Mueller/Shutterstock; 12BC, © majeczka/Shutterstock; 12BR, © Humbak/Shutterstock; 13, © Marilyn Barbone/Shutterstock; 14TL, © Heiko Kiera/Shutterstock; 14BL, © Tom Vezo/Naturepl; 14BR, © Anne Kitzman/Shutterstock; 15, © Image Source/Corbis; 16TL, © Geoffrey Kuchera/Shutterstock; 16B, © Naturfoto-Online/Alamy; 17, © operative401/Shutterstock; 18L, © mffoto/Shutterstock; 18R, © Roger Tidman/FLPA; 19, © Claude Nuridsany & Marie Perennou/Science Photo Library; 20L, © Irin-K/Shutterstock; 20B, © Jaimie Duplass/Shutterstock; 21L, © AlgarsR/Shutterstock; 21R, © Blend Images/Superstock; 22, © Shutterstock; 23TL, © Michael Pettigrew/Shutterstock; 23TC, © psamtik/Shutterstock; 23TR, © mffoto/Shutterstock; 23BL, © Doug Lemke/Shutterstock; 23BC, © Loskutnikov/Shutterstock; 23BR, © Andrey Armyagov/Shutterstock.

Publisher: Kenn Goin
Senior Editor: Lisa Wiseman
Creative Director: Spencer Brinker
Design: Emma Randall
Editor: Mark J. Sachner
Photo Researcher: Ruby Tuesday Books Ltd.

Library of Congress Cataloging-in-Publication Data

Owen, Ruth, 1967-
  How do you know it's summer? / by Ruth Owen.
    p. cm. — (Signs of the seasons)
  Includes bibliographical references and index.
  ISBN-13: 978-1-61772-399-5 (library binding)
  ISBN-10: 1-61772-399-1 (library binding)
  1. Summer—Juvenile literature. I. Title.
  QB637.6.O94 2012
  508.2—dc23

                    2011044571

For more information, write to Bearport Publishing Company, Inc., 45 West 21st Street, Suite 3B, New York, New York 10010. Printed in the United States of America in North Mankato, Minnesota.

10 9 8 7 6 5 4 3 2 1

Contents

It's Summer!

There are four seasons in every year—spring, summer, fall, and winter.

Summer is the season when many people have fun at the beach on hot sunny days.

Gardens are filled with colorful flowers.

Busy **insects** seem to be everywhere.

Look for these and other signs of summer as spring comes to an end each year.

June

Su	M	T	W	Th	F	Sa
					1	2
3	4	5	6	7	8	9
10	11	12	13	14	15	16
17	18	19	20	21	22	23
24	25	26	27	28	29	30

first day of summer

Each year, summer starts on either June 20 or June 21. The first day of summer is marked on calendars.

4

Describe what summer weather is like where you live.

5

The Longest Day Is Here

As summer gets closer, there are more hours of light each day.

Sometimes it is even still light outside at bedtime!

The first day of summer is the longest day of the year.

This means there are many more hours of light than darkness on that day.

Once summer arrives and the longest day has passed, there are fewer hours of daylight each day.

It's Heating Up

Hot **weather** is often a sign that summer has arrived.

It may even feel hot outside at night!

In some places it may not rain for days or weeks during the summer.

kids cooling off

In some places, summer is the time for thunderstorms. People may see lightning flashes and hear the rumble of thunder.

Every Saturday for four weeks during the summer, use a thermometer to measure the temperature outside. Each measurement must be done at the same time of day. See how the temperature changes from week to week.

Weather chart

Date	Temperature
June 22	65°F (18°C)
June 29	67°F (19°C)
July 6	72°F (22°C)
July 13	80°F (27°C)

Summer Colors

Many plants grow colorful flowers in summertime.

Butterflies and bees often go from flower to flower to find food.

They are looking for the sweet liquid that flowers make.

It is called **nectar**.

Plants make **seeds** inside their flowers. The seeds drop from the flowers in late summer and fall. In spring the seeds will grow into new plants.

Different types of flowers have different colors and smells. Smell several different kinds of flowers. Then draw a picture of each flower in a notebook. Write down words that describe each flower's smell under each picture.

a bee looking for nectar

11

Green Leaves

In spring, fat green **buds** grow on the branches of some trees.

The buds burst open into flowers and leaves.

By summer, however, the flowers have disappeared and the leaves cover the trees.

There may be another clue that summer has arrived hidden among the leaves—fruit!

On apple trees, for example, tiny apples begin to appear during summer.

bud

apple tree flowers

apple tree leaves

tiny apples

Many insects and spiders live in trees. Look for them on the trunk of a tree or on branches and leaves close to the ground. Check the area around the tree, too. Count how many bugs you see. Don't touch or disturb the tiny creatures.

The leaves of a tree make a shady spot where people and animals can cool off on a hot day.

shade

13

Time to Leave Home

Summer is the season when many young animals leave their mothers.

Squirrels are born in spring.

By the summer they are old enough to live on their own.

They will build themselves homes, called dreys, from twigs and leaves.

squirrel

a squirrel collecting twigs and leaves

drey

14

In summer, it is usually cooler in the early morning and evening than in the middle of the day. Many animals look for food at these times. They rest in the shade during the hottest parts of the day.

Taking Off!

Many young birds learn to fly in summer.

For example, a swallow chick begins to learn by standing on the edge of its nest.

It flaps its little wings again and again, trying them out.

Then it jumps!

With its mother and father close by, the young swallow takes its first flying lesson.

young swallow

nest

Birds like to splash in water to cool off in the summer.

a bird taking a bath

Put about two inches (5 cm) of water in a shallow bowl and leave it outside. Then watch for about 15 minutes and count how many birds come by to cool off in the water.

Tiny Signs of Summer

In summer, you can see more insects than at any other time of year!

Grasshoppers hop around on lawns, eating grass and other plants.

Tiny **aphids** suck the juices from plants.

Hungry ladybugs stay busy eating the aphids!

grasshopper

black ants eating a melon

Look for black ants in your backyard. If you see some, put out three piles of food—lettuce, sugar, and bread crumbs. Guess which food the ants will like best. Watch to see if you guessed right.

ladybug

aphids

Insects eat plants and other insects! In summer, it is easy for them to find lots of food.

19

Summer in a Garden

In summer, the seeds that people planted in spring have grown into plants.

Giant sunflowers soar taller than a child!

Juicy red tomatoes hang from tomato plants.

Crunchy carrots grow under the soil.

Summer is the season when gardens are filled with flowers and good things to eat.

sunflower

tomatoes

Summer lasts until September 22 or 23. Then fall begins!

carrots

Science Lab

When you are playing in your backyard, on the playground at school, or in the park, go on a summer treasure hunt.

See how many of the things on the Summer Treasure Hunt list you can see, smell, hear, or collect.

If it's not summer where you live, then draw a picture of summer.

Include as many things from the list as you can.

Then when summer comes to where you live, go outside and try to find the things you put in your drawing.

Summer Treasure Hunt

Things to see

A ladybug

A butterfly

Ants going into and out of a crack in the pavement

An animal under a shady tree

A bird taking a bath

Fruit growing on a tree

A flower that is taller than you

Things to smell

Freshly mown grass

The air after it has rained on a hot day

Things to hear

The chirping of crickets

A bee buzzing

A bird chirping

Things to collect

Five green leaves with different shapes

A blue flower

A red flower

Science Words

aphids (AY-fids) small insects that eat the juices of plants

buds (BUHDZ) small growths on the stems of trees and other plants that grow into flowers and leaves

insects (IN-sekts) small animals that have six legs, three main body parts, two antennas, and a hard covering called an exoskeleton

nectar (NEK-tur) a sweet liquid made by plants

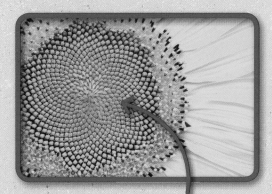

seeds (SEEDZ) tiny parts of a plant that form in the flower and can grow into a new plant

weather (WETH-ur) how hot or cold it is outside, and other conditions such as rain, wind, and snow

Index

Read More

Branley, Franklyn M. *Sunshine Makes the Seasons (Let's-Read-and-Find-Out Science).* New York: HarperCollins (2005).

Glaser, Linda. *It's Summer! (Celebrate the Seasons).* Minneapolis, MN: Millbrook Press (2003).

Kalman, Bobbie, and Kelley MacAulay. *Changing Seasons.* New York: Crabtree Publishing (2005).

Learn More Online

To learn more about summer, visit **www.bearportpublishing.com/SignsoftheSeasons**

About the Author

Ruth Owen has been developing, editing, and writing children's books for more than ten years. She particularly enjoys working on books about animals and the natural world. Ruth lives in Cornwall, England, just minutes from the ocean. She loves gardening and caring for her family of llamas.